This Is a Let's-Read-and-Find-Out Science Book ®

ROCK COLLECTING

by Roma Gans

illustrated by Holly Keller

HarperCollins*Publishers*

Other Let's-Read-and-Find-Out Science Books® You Will Enjoy

A Drop of Blood • Air Is All Around You • An Octopus Is Amazing • Ant Cities • The Beginning of the Earth • The Big Dipper • Comets • Danger—Icebergs! • Digging Up Dinosaurs • Dinosaur Bones • Dinosaurs Are Different • Ducks Don't Get Wet • Ears Are for Hearing • Earthquakes • Eclipse: Darkness in Daytime • Evolution • Feel the Wind • Fireflies in the Night • Flash, Crash, Rumble, and Roll • Follow the Water from Brook to Ocean • Fossils Tell of Long Ago • Germs Make Me Sick! • Get Ready for Robots! • Glaciers • Gravity Is a Mystery • How a Seed Grows • How Do Apples Grow? • How Many Teeth? • How We Learned the Earth Is Round • How You Talk • Hurricane Watch • I'm Growing! • Is There Life in Outer Space? • Journey into a Black Hole • The Moon Seems to Change • My Hands • My Feet • My Five Senses • My Visit to the Dinosaurs • The Planets in Our Solar System • Rock Collecting • Rockets and Satellites • Shooting Stars • The Skeleton Inside You • Snakes Are Hunters • Snow Is Falling • The Sun: Our Nearest Star • Sunshine Makes the Seasons • Switch On, Switch Off • Tornado Alert • Volcanoes • What Happened to the Dinosaurs? • What Happens to a Hamburger • What Makes Day and Night • What the Moon Is Like • What Will the Weather Be? • Your Skin and Mine

The *Let's-Read-and-Find-Out Science Book* series was originated by Dr. Franklyn M. Branley, Astronomer Emeritus and former Chairman of the American Museum-Hayden Planetarium, and was formerly coedited by him and Dr. Roma Gans, Professor Emeritus of Childhood Education, Teachers College, Columbia University. For a complete catalog of Let's-Read-and-Find-Out Science Books, write to HarperCollins Children's Books, 10 East 53rd Street, New York, NY 10022.

Photo credits: American Museum of Natural History, N.Y., 7 (right), 12, 13, 18, 22, 25; Floyd R. Getsinger, 7 (left), 14, 15.

Library of Congress Cataloging-in-Publication Data
Gans, Roma, 1894-
    Rock collecting.

    (Let's-read-and-find-out science book)
    Summary: Explains how to start a rock collection and how to recognize igneous, metamorphic, and sedimentary rocks.
    1. Rocks—Collectors and collecting—Juvenile literature. [1. Rocks—Collectors and collecting] II. Keller, Holly, ill. II. Title. III. Series.
QE433.6 G.36 1984   552′.0075   83-46170
ISBN 0-690-04265-5
ISBN 0-690-04266-3 (lib. bdg.)

ROCK COLLECTING

13.89

People collect all kinds of things. They collect coins, stamps, baseball cards, shells, toys, bottles, pictures, and cats. Some people collect things that are very old—the older the better.

The oldest things you can collect are rocks. Most of them are millions and millions of years old.

One way to start a collection is to look for rocks of different colors. You'll find there are pink rocks, black rocks, and pure white ones. There are gray rocks, and brown and yellow ones.

Most kinds of rocks are easy to find. But some, like diamonds and emeralds, are rare. That's why they are valuable.

3

Thousands of years ago the Romans built roads
out of rocks. The roads are still used today.

THESE HUGE BLOCKS
WERE CUT FROM
LIMESTONE

Five thousand years ago the Egyptians built the

pyramids with rocks. They are still standing.

Maybe someday you'll go to Egypt and see them.

Some rocks are soft, much too soft to build with. Talc is so soft you can pinch it into powder with your fingers.

Talc is number one on the scale for hardness of rocks. The scale goes from 1 to 10. Diamonds are number 10. They are the hardest rocks in the world.

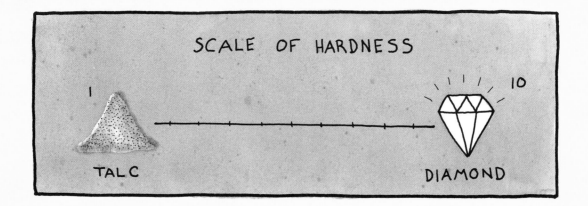

talc

diamond

Rocks cover the whole earth. No matter where you live, you live on rock.

There is rock under city streets and country farms. And there is rock under every ocean, lake, and river.

The rocks that cover the surface of the earth are called the earth's crust. Most of the crust is made of igneous rock. Igneous means made by heat.

Inside the earth it is very hot—hot enough to melt rock. The melted rock is called magma.

Sometimes the magma pushes through cracks in the crust. When magma comes to the surface it is called lava. The lava cools and becomes very hard. It becomes igneous rock.

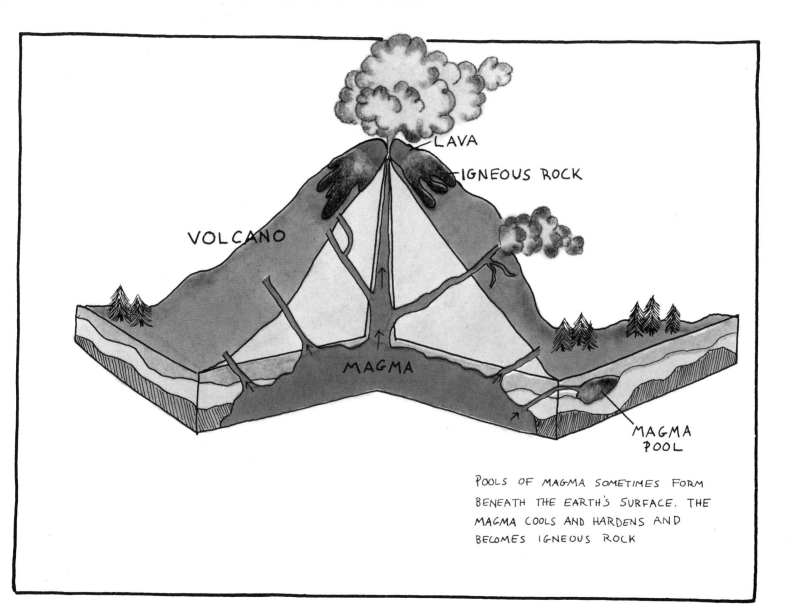

POOLS OF MAGMA SOMETIMES FORM
BENEATH THE EARTH'S SURFACE. THE
MAGMA COOLS AND HARDENS AND
BECOMES IGNEOUS ROCK

Granite is an igneous rock. It once was magma. Some granite is gray with small, shiny black and white crystals. Some granite has large pink, black, and white crystals.

Quartz is another igneous rock. It is hard—
number 7 on the scale of hardness. Some pieces of
quartz are white like milk. Others are clear like
glass.

Sometimes quartz has bands of many colors. Jewelry is made from it. The marbles you play with may be made of banded quartz.

Basalt is another kind of igneous rock. It is
usually dark in color—gray, green, or black. It is the
most common of all igneous rocks.

Not all rocks are igneous rocks. Some are made of sediments. Sandstone is one kind of sedimentary rock. It is made of grains of sand.

Millions of years ago, sand was blown into rivers. The rivers carried the sand along and dropped it into lakes or oceans. Layer after layer settled on the bottoms of the lakes and seas. The top layers pressed down on the bottom layers. Slowly the lower layers of sand became stone.

SEDIMENTARY ROCK FORMING

You'll know sandstone when you see it. It is soft and grainy. Rub it with your fingers, and grains of sand will come off.

Shale is another kind of sedimentary rock. Clay
is the sediment it is made of. Shale is used to
make cement. Cement is used to make concrete for
sidewalks.

Another sedimentary rock is limestone. It is made of the shells of animals that lived millions of years ago. Most often, limestone is white. But it can be pink, tan, and other colors. Sometimes you can see the outlines of shells in limestone.

The chalk you write with is limestone.

Limestone is also used to make cement.

LIMESTONE AND CLAY

The lime used on lawns and gardens is usually ground-up limestone.

LIME

FOR GREENER GRASS AND TREES

The third kind of rock in the earth's crust is called metamorphic. Metamorphic means changed.

Slate is a metamorphic rock. Slate was once shale. But over millions of years, tons and tons of rock pressed down on it. The pressure made the shale very hot, and the heat and pressure changed it into slate.

Chalkboards are made of slate.

SHALE
+ HEAT
+ PRESSURE
—————
SLATE

Slate is sometimes
used to cover the
roofs of buildings.

Most slate is gray, but some is black, red, or brown.

Other metamorphic rocks are made the same way slate is, by heat and pressure. Some metamorphic rocks are so changed you can't tell what they once were.

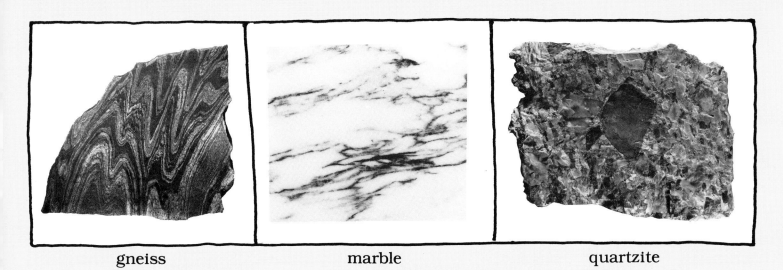

gneiss   marble   quartzite

Granite turns into gneiss. It once was a piece of gray granite. Now it is darker gray, and the crystals in it have separated into layers.

Limestone turns into marble. Some marble has colored marks that look like clouds.

Sandstone turns into quartzite. It may still look like sedimentary sandstone. But now it is much harder.

When you start collecting rocks, you'll find
out how many different varieties there are.
See if you can tell if they are igneous rocks,
sedimentary rocks, or metamorphic rocks.

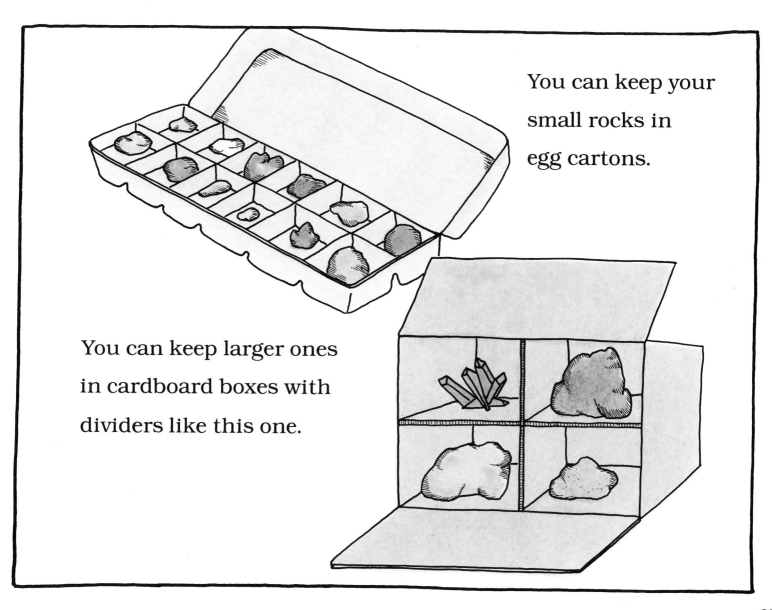

You can keep your
small rocks in
egg cartons.

You can keep larger ones
in cardboard boxes with
dividers like this one.

Rock collecting is fun. And one of the best things about it is you can do it anywhere. Wherever you go, try to find new rocks and add them to your collection.